PEARLS
ON THE PATH

MAHAMANDALESHWAR SWAMI
NITYANANDA

ISBN 978-0-9886025-0-2

Shanti Mandir
51 Muktananda Marg
Walden, NY 12586, U.S.A.

Tel: +1 (845) 778 – 1008
www.shantimandir.com

TABLE OF CONTENTS

PREFACE

IN THE LAST FEW YEARS of his life, great *avadhūt* Bhagavān Nityānanda spoke very little. But it is said that a few days before his *mahāsamādhi*, on the occasion of Guru Pūrṇimā, he spoke for about forty-five minutes.

His exact words weren't recorded, but the gist of what he said has been passed down: "What sort of grace can be bestowed on someone who, when one desire has been granted, immediately seeks fulfillment of another? Such a person does not need a Guru but a soothsayer."

According to Bhagavān, such people were merely window shopping. "They came to the ocean only to catch a few readily available fish," he said, "not to dive deep for the pearls lying below."

I myself saw that Baba Muktānanda, after years of working with people, after twelve years of travelling around the world, was disgusted at some of what he saw happening around him.

People ask me, "How can you call a great being disgusted? A great being lives in a state of equilibrium at all times."

Of course, such a being has great compassion, and that compassion compels him to do the work he does. If this isn't the case, of all fools I am the greatest. Why? Because I have an

BHAGAVĀN NITYĀNANDA

ashram and I let everybody come. I try to make sure everybody goes home happy and content.

Yet I always remember what Bhagavān said, and how I found
Baba at the end of his life. Yes, I'm sure Bhagavān had great
contentment, as did Baba, knowing he was able to awaken
people from their ignorance. Yet sadness came from the fact
that he had pearls, as Bhagavān said, to offer, but everybody
was content with the fish on the top.

Just a little bit of peace, a little bit of bliss, a little bit of happiness—that is only the surface. We must dive deeper within
ourselves, we must become established in the knowledge of
the Truth.

— *Mahāmandaleśvar Swami Nityānanda*

1

MEDITATION IS A WAY OF LIFE

MEDITATION is awareness of the moment.

Many people think if you turn the lights off, sit in your perfect posture, say some mantras, and your mind becomes blank, that is meditation.

The philosophy of Shaivism says the state of meditation, called *turīya*, has to be like the uninterrupted flow of oil that is poured from one can to another.

Whether you're in the waking state, dream state, or deep sleep state, meditation goes on continuously. You are at peace when you are working or talking to somebody. You're still at peace when you are dreaming or in deep sleep. That stillness, that peace, does not go away.

This is what meditation is. It's an art. It's a way of life. You don't try to induce a state or go into a particular state. Rather, it is about acceptance and just being.

2

SHANTI MANDIR IS YOU

ŚĀNTI means peace. *Mandir* means temple.

The body is a temple. Therefore, Shanti Mandir is *you*. It is all the people who come to satsaṅg, because each one is a temple of peace.

Even if you think you are the body, within you dwells divinity. This is not just a physical body, it is a body in which God dwells. Therefore, you are that temple.

If you treat your body with this understanding, then you will understand Baba Muktānanda's message "worship your Self, kneel to your Self, honor your Self."

3

LOVE FOR THE SAKE OF THE SELF

THE MIND DOUBTS, thinking, "How can I know for sure that God dwells in this body?"

After all, scientific proof demands we measure it empirically. But Consciousness is not something to be measured objectively. It can only be known subjectively, within one's own heart.

When someone we love dies, we can't wait to do the final rites and get rid of the body. Why? Because the one we loved is no longer in that body. Without life, without the presence of the soul in the body, it will simply rot. When that inner divinity has departed, we no longer love the body of five elements. If we did, we would keep it forever.

This is why, in the *Upaniṣads*, the sage Yājñavalkya says to his wife, Maitreyī, "We do not love each other for our own sake. We love each other for the sake of the Self."

Of course, when death comes, we don't see Consciousness depart unless our inner eye is open. We simply think individual existence has come to an end. But it is only the body that has come to an end. The individual, in the form of Consciousness, goes on.

4

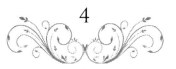

THE SĀDHANĀ IS ŚIVA, AND THE ATTAINMENT IS ŚIVA

WHEREAS THE PHILOSOPHY of Vedānta talks about the Absolute as Brahman, Shaivism talks about the Absolute as Śiva. Shaivism says to think of yourself as Śiva, knowing the goal you want to attain is Śiva and the path to get there is Śiva.

That path—what you do between where you are now and your goal—is called *sādhanā*, spiritual practices.

Shaivism says there is no difference between you, the sādhanā you do, and the goal.

Contemplate this. When you realize that you are Śiva, that the sādhanā you do is Śiva, and that the goal is Śiva, then there is nothing to do. There is nothing to be done, and therefore there is nothing to be attained. Understand this notion?

You already are Śiva, so there is no sādhanā to be done. At the same time, because sādhanā is also Śiva, you do it. It's not just that you do chanting or meditation, you do Śiva. When you realize this, then you are not doing Śiva anymore because that is the state of Śiva.

We tend to meditate with the understanding "I have to attain something. Therefore, I, Nityānanda, am going to meditate to find and experience Śiva." When we realize "I am not this person, Nityānanda, but I am Śiva," that is called meditation. We also call it the Absolute. We call it Consciousness, Truth.

So, Shaivism says, "I am Śiva, the sādhanā I am doing is Śiva, and the attainment is Śiva." This understanding removes the concept of effort, of thinking, "I, Nityānanda, am going to give up my limited identity to become that which is great and vast."

What we do is allow ourselves to become one. We are already one, but we allow ourselves to once again become aware of the oneness between us and that which we call God.

5

SANĀTANA DHARMA

BEFORE THE WORD *Hinduism* was coined, the philosophy of our tradition was known as *sanātana dharma*. Dharma means the law that sustains life. Sanātana means eternal.

We believe that the Hindu philosophy, which has existed for many thousands of years, was not created by any particular individual.

Our duty as Mahāmandaleśvars, as Gurus, of this philosophical tradition is to make sure the teachings of the *Vedas* are kept alive, allowing people to become aware that they must live a good, righteous, honest, and straightforward life.

Living according to the teachings of the *Vedas* might seem hard in today's world. Yet if we try, I believe this will give us a happy, peaceful life.

6

ANCIENT TEACHINGS FOR
A MODERN WORLD

IN THIS SO-CALLED MODERN TIME, people wonder about the value of ancient rituals. They think, "What is the purpose of these rituals when in other ways we've become so modern?"

But think about what modern society has to offer. It has offered us sickness and mental suffering and all the various problems associated with that. We may think we have progressed, but we must ask in what way we have moved ahead. Children born today are no happier than children born thirty, forty, fifty years ago.

The teachings the sages gave thousands of years ago are applicable today. These teachings show us how to follow dharma, right conduct, and how to live according to what is talked about in the scriptures.

We may think we need something new, a way to entertain the mind. But those entertainments only last for a time, and then the mind craves something else. Instead, follow the teachings that have been handed down for generations and that have borne fruit for others.

Through contemplation, discrimination, and understanding, find what works for you, practice it, and let it bear fruit for you, too.

7

R&D ON THE HUMAN SITUATION

RECENTLY SOMEBODY SAID, "I know everything is Brahman. I am Brahman. So why all these trappings? Why so many kinds of rituals and practices?"

The mind decides, "What I like is fine. What I don't like is a trapping."

Imagine you have a headache and you go to the doctor. The doctor says, "Take Pepto-Bismol." You go to the same doctor with a cut. The doctor grinds up Pepto-Bismol and puts it on. Would you think that doctor is smart?

You'd think, "I want a doctor who knows what medications should be prescribed for different ailments."

Researchers in the R&D department of a company try to find products that will work for different situations. In the same way, yogis and sages sat in the jungles, in the forests, in their ashrams and did R&D on the human situation.

The wise man gives us different prescriptions that apply to our different mental situations. In the *Bhagavad Gītā*, Lord Kṛṣṇa tells Arjuna, "Follow the path the scriptures have laid out." By following these teachings, you will slowly rid yourself of negative tendencies.

8

TRAIN YOURSELF TO SIT

FOR MEDITATION, the very first thing to do is to sit properly.

People always say, "But how can I sit still?"

If you don't practice, you get so used to fiddling, moving, scratching an itch, worrying about your shawl or about this and that, that your mind is constantly distracted.

Teach yourself to sit. Practice sitting still. Of course, there will be pain. There will be messages from the body. But if you gradually train yourself, you'll find you can sit.

The more active or excited the mind is, the harder it is to sit still. The stiller and quieter the mind becomes, the easier it is to sit. See if you can become aware of this.

9

PRĀṆĀYĀMA

THE MIND AND BREATH are interrelated. When we breathe fast, the mind thinks fast. But we can slow the breath down.

One of the practices yoga teaches is *prāṇāyāma*, control of the breath.

There are many kinds of prāṇāyāma. One simple technique is to first observe the natural flow of the breath. Notice how your breath is usually rapid and shallow.

Then allow the exhalations and inhalations to become longer. As the breath goes longer on the exhalation and longer on the inhalation, the mind becomes quieter.

As each breath is released, allow it to flush out the mind. Let the thoughts go. Then take in fresh air, and again release.

You can do this during the day when you find yourself caught in the midst of things. Take a moment to focus your attention on your third eye, the space between the eyebrows, and breathe for maybe two minutes. You will find what a difference it makes. It brings you to your center.

Learn to be centered at all times—when you get hurt, when you get angry, when you get upset, when you hate, when you love. Then everything you do and say comes from a space of light. You may not always be able to stay centered, but whenever you truly connect with your center, then whatever you do comes from that place of Truth.

The yogic scriptures say we may not be able to directly control the mind, but by gaining control over the breath we can gain control over the mind.

10

DISCARD WHAT IS USELESS

WHEN WE BECOME established in sitting, we are aware that our mind has many thoughts.

Train your mind throughout the day to have as few thoughts as possible. Discard useless thoughts.

Just as you fill your wastepaper basket with things you don't want, teach yourself not to keep that which is useless in your life.

When you are surrounded with only useful things, your mind can focus. What do you focus upon? Focus on each action you perform. Become clear about that action, and focus upon it.

11

JOY

A MILLION DOLLARS may bring you joy.

But as soon as the million dollars are gone, you have to run back to Vegas or Atlantic City.

That which is truly good will always stay with you. Joy doesn't depend on any external source. It comes from your very own heart.

12

THE MIND KEEPS US BOUND

IT IS SAID in the scriptures that when God first created this earth, He gave humans the understanding that if they wanted to come back to the Absolute, they could come back.

Of course, that would never work. As soon as a person had the thought "This is not fun!" he would simply merge back into the Absolute.

Therefore, God had to create a means by which humans would keep themselves going.

Any scripture you read talks very little about God. It talks about the mind. Because the mind is the one thing that always keeps us going.

Even if I say something now, you think, "Do I agree with him? Maybe, maybe not."

Only when you have experiences of peace and joy beyond the mind do you get a little taste of freedom. Until then, you are bound by the mind. All you know is the creation of your mind.

If I live in India, I can probably imagine what America is like. But if I'm in America, I know what it is. When we've had our own direct experience, we can know and say, "This is what I want."

The sages tell us we are slaves of the mind. When we go beyond the mind, we are no longer its slave. Instead, the mind is our slave. If we want to think, the mind will think.

Now if I say, "We'll sit quietly," you may sit externally quietly, but the mind may still be going. Ultimately, you get to a point where you are able to say, "I want to be quiet." It's like turning off a switch so the mind can become quiet. When you've had that experience, you know what it is to be free.

13

EACH THOUGHT MAKES A RIPPLE

IN MEDITATION, as you focus on your breath, you become aware of all the various things that cause disturbance in your mind.

Imagine a pond. Somebody is standing at the edge and tossing pebbles into the still water. The water starts to make ripples. The first stone, the second stone, the third stone, the fourth stone—each makes more ripples.

Similarly, when the mind is still, each thought makes a ripple. More thoughts mean many ripples. And when those thoughts combine with emotions, they are like great lumps of dirt rising from the bottom of the pond.

If the mind is agitated, any emotion that arises acts as fuel. But if the mind is not agitated, that emotion dissipates after a period of time.

People ask, "How can I control my jealousy? How can I control my anger?"

In the second chapter of the *Bhagavad Gītā,* Lord Kṛṣṇa says such a person must not allow himself to be disturbed by the thoughts that cause ripples in his mind.

This is what we want to do in meditation. We want to understand our mind so that when emotions arise, the mind is not affected by them. Let the mind be still. Let the mind be steady. Let the mind be focused.

14

CLEAN THE MIND LAYER BY LAYER

RECENTLY I WAS IN MEXICO and somebody asked, "How long does it take to clean the mind?'

The hall there has large windows, so I said, "How long it takes to clean a window depends on how dirty the window is. Then, depending on how much dirt comes into the room, you have to constantly work to keep it clean."

I said, "When you first see the dirt on the window, you think, 'This is going to be a lot of work!' You work quickly, and soon you say, 'Okay, it's clean now.' But then you step back and look more carefully. You see it's not really clean. Just the first layer has been cleaned."

You can apply the same concept to meditation. Except you can't see how clean the mind has become; you have to know that.

At first as you observe yourself, there are only minor changes. The top layer has been cleaned. Gradually, as you meditate, the senses come under your control. Instead of your mind constantly thinking, "I want this, I want this, I want this," it begins to enjoy that which it has.

15

KNOWLEDGE IS WITHIN

AS HUMANS with minds and egos, we want to understand everything. But if you look at the life you have lived for so many years, how much do you really understand about it?

For example, how do you go to sleep? What is the actual process that happens? You've been sleeping since you were a little one, yet you still don't know how you sleep. And what is it that wakes you up in the morning?

If we don't understand these matters that are related to the body, how can we begin to comprehend everything the sages are trying to explain?

Nevertheless, as we chant, as we worship, the meaning of these practices comes of its own accord. Knowledge arises from within us.

16

TALK TO YOUR REFLECTION

WE DON'T ALWAYS KNOW what is happening within us. Of course we do know, yet we think we don't.

So what I suggest is to find a mirror. I'm sure you have a small mirror in your purse, or wallet, or somewhere.

Look at the person you see in the mirror, and smile back at that person. Or you can frown and then go, "No, no, I don't like that frown," and instead smile back.

Of course, it's a reflection. Have a conversation with that reflection.

You can say, "Nityānanda, smile."

When that Nityānanda smiles, this Nityānanda is smiling. Hence that Nityānanda also is smiling. Then the "I," the ātman, looks and says, "Hey, Nityānanda, you're smiling."

And he goes, "Yes, I'm smiling."

So you tell him, "Keep smiling."

It's good fun. All of a sudden you are the witness watching this reflection and talking to it, but actually you are talking to yourself. You are fooling your own mind.

THE SOUND OF GOD

ACCORDING TO the philosophy of Shaivism, all this that we see as forms, as solid mass, is nothing but vibrations of the sound energy of God. It is the sound *Oṁ*.

When you put your ear to a conch shell, you hear the sound of the ocean. You hear *Oṁ* in that conch shell.

Everything in this world is filled with sound. Through mantra we can connect to that sound in its subtlest form.

18

LET YOUR MIND VIBRATE WITH *OṀ*

THE WORD *mantra* is formed of two Sanskrit words, *man* and *tra*. *Man* is the mind, and *tra* is that which redeems us, which frees us from the mind.

If we want to experience sound at its deepest level, we have to switch the mind from all our petty thoughts to sound in the form of God.

The same mind that is vibrating now with all these thoughts—"I like this, I like that, I hate this, I hate that"— must vibrate instead with the sound of God at all times.

19

MANTRA IS THE VEHICLE

WHY DO WE REPEAT the name of God? We do it because the mind has a tendency to think.

Just telling the mind to be quiet usually isn't enough to make it become quiet. The mind needs something to focus upon. It needs a tool. The mantra is such a tool.

Baba often likened the mantra to a car. A car is a vehicle that brings you to your destination, to your home. When you arrive at the destination, you leave the vehicle and enter your house.

20

A HORSE IS A HORSE

MANY WORDS came into existence a long time ago. We believe a horse is a horse because everybody calls it a horse.

In the same way, on the spiritual path, the master teaches us to repeat a mantra that has been used for a long time.

By constant repetition and contemplation of this mantra, the master came to the experience of Truth within himself. By giving the mantra to us, he tries to convey and share the experience of Truth.

21

TRUTH

TRUTH IS THE EXPERIENCE we have when we are happy and content, when nothing needs to be said. We feel full. We don't want anything from anyone, we are just here.

We need do nothing except recognize that Truth is present in our life.

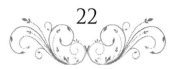

22

LET THE MANTRA OVERPOWER YOUR THOUGHTS

WHAT IS THE DIFFERENCE between a ten watt and a twenty-five watt and a hundred watt light bulb? They all look the same, and the electricity going to them is the same, but the capacity of each bulb is different.

In the same way, when it comes to repeating the mantra, each individual is different. How much of the mantra's power I can hold, how much you can hold, and how much someone else can hold will be different. Depending on our capacity, we receive a different "wattage" from the mantra.

Right now, your thoughts might be burning at a hundred-and-fifty watts and the mantra at twenty-five watts. So the brightness of the thoughts overpowers that of the mantra. As you continue to practice, slowly the glow of the thoughts diminishes and that of the mantra increases.

The mantra we receive from the Guru ignites a flame within us.

That can feel like two-hundred volts have been put into a one-hundred volt bulb. For a moment it's okay, but if it continues the bulb will burn out.

We have received knowledge, but we don't know how to hold it. So we yearn for that experience again. We feel, "I want that peace, that joy."

The Guru says, "You can have it. But you must do these practices and get yourself there."

Getting ourselves there means purifying the mind, purifying the ego, cleansing ourselves. We do *japa*, repetition of the mantra, and other practices so we can hold that state.

23

LET JAPA GO TO THE HEART

THE SAGES GIVE us a technique for doing japa using a *mālā* of beads.

Place your ring finger and thumb together, and use the middle finger to move the beads. Not the first finger, the middle finger. This makes a direct connection to the heart.

You may have seen a priest putting his beads inside a bag. The sages recommend this. Because otherwise somebody might watch you and think, "He's doing japa," and thus cast a subtle bad thought on you.

We tend to think of bad thoughts as bad in the sense of being negative or wrong. But even if somebody looks at you and says, "How beautiful," there can be a tinge of jealousy behind that thought.

Immediately your ego feels good that somebody said, "How beautiful." But later you feel a shift in yourself, a change in your energy. You begin to wonder, "Is there a stain on my clothes? Has my necklace moved? Is my makeup spoiled?" But really it is that unspoken jealousy behind the "how beautiful."

Therefore, the sages say it is best to practice in our own space, and to do it quietly. When you do japa, do it beneath a cloth or inside a bag.

Do it near the heart. You want the mantra to go directly into the heart because that is the space where the mind resides within this body.

24

A MILLION REPETITIONS

IN INDIA, there is a tradition to do a hundred thousand, five-hundred thousand, or a million repetitions of the mantra. The scriptures state how many repetitions one should do each day to arrive at the hundred thousand or the million.

Some people who have read this in a scripture think if they do a million repetitions they will get it. So they count whenever they do japa. Then they say, "I've done so much!" Or "I've only got so many more to go…"

Whatever I might say won't enlighten them in that moment because they are looking forward to the end of those two-hundred thousand repetitions remaining. So I laugh to myself and think, "Then what? You'll be more frustrated because at the end of those million repetitions you won't find yourself any different than you were when you started at number one."

That is not to say a million repetitions of the mantra would not make a difference. Of course it would. It would make you realize that a million repetitions don't do anything unless you understand what you are doing.

Others pick up their mālā at different times during the day and do a few repetitions, then put it down and go about their business. They pick up, do it, put it down. The sages discourage this because one is neither doing what one is supposed to be doing nor really doing japa.

Of course, you might argue, "Isn't that better than doing nothing?"

I think it is best to focus on your work, finish your work, and then find fifteen minutes for japa. During those fifteen minutes, focus totally upon the mantra.

25

PRATYĀHĀRA

PRATYĀHĀRA, withdrawal of the senses, is a very important practice for meditation and for life. The mind, through the senses, races to the outside world. As the senses are drawn into the world, always remember to bring them back.

Sleep is nothing but a form of pratyāhāra. All our senses are withdrawn when we go to sleep. But sleep is an unconscious state. In sleep, we aren't aware of all that is going on around us.

When we perform pratyāhāra in a conscious manner, consciously withdrawing the senses, we find that we begin to experience contentment. We begin to experience peace and joy.

In meditation, we want to reach *samādhi*, total absorption in the divine. First, however, we must be content. If there is no experience of contentment, we can't sit still, we can't become focused, we can't turn within.

So the first thing we must learn is to be content with who we are, content with what we have, content with life, content with everything going on around us.

CLOSE THE DOORS OF THE SENSES

WHEN WE LOOK at an object, it is not the eye but the mind through the eye that perceives that object. It is also through the mind that the eye enjoys the object. The eye is just the sense organ, the door, through which the mind enjoys what is seen.

The same is true for sound. The ear is the door through which the mind enjoys sound. Similarly, the nose is the door through which the mind enjoys smell. The mouth is the door through which the mind enjoys taste.

In meditation, we want to close these doors so the mind takes in less.

Many people think, "For an hour I'll sit quietly with the doors of the senses closed, but for the other twenty-three hours all the doors will remain open and working."

Then they come to me and say, "I used to believe in all this meditation, but now I don't."

Imagine you're in a cold room and you turn the heating system on, and at the same time you open all the doors and windows. And then you complain the room isn't getting hot.

Anybody who comes along would laugh and say, "Close the doors!"

But you say, "No, I also like to feel the cold air."

When people sit for an hour of meditation but leave the doors of the senses wide open all the rest of the time, they can't fault meditation. I tell such people, "If you close the doors, it might work." But not everybody wants to listen.

27

A STRONG MIND

WHEN I TRAVEL the world and visit people's homes, I see that the first thing they do when they wake up is turn on the radio.

I ask, "Why?"

They say, "To wake myself up!"

They have become dependent on somebody else to wake them up. How can such a weak mind expect itself to meditate?

First the mind needs to become strong.

As the mind gains strength, slowly our senses come under our control. When we have control at all times, we experience *manaḥprasādaḥ*, cheerfulness of mind. We receive the blessings of the mind. Only then can we go deep in meditation.

28

BECOME THE WITNESS
OF YOUR MIND

WE SHOULDN'T CONDEMN the mind. The mind is the greatest asset given by God because the mind is that which is able to discriminate between the Truth and what is merely the experience we are having in this moment.

The *Upaniṣads* say that what we want to experience is what powers the mind. God is not that which is thought of by the mind; God is that by which the mind thinks.

We want to get to the source of the mind.

When we get to the source, we can have fun with life. We don't regret doing anything we do. We don't have to feel unhappy or depressed or sad, because we have learned how to become a witness.

29

LIVE WITH EXUBERANCE

WHEN WE LIVE with exuberance, with joy, with zest, with passion, all of life seems filled with that. There is joy on the face. The body exudes peace. Everything is great. Everything goes smoothly.

But when we live in fear, life seems filled with anxiety and pitfalls. When we are down, all we do is gripe and complain. We say, "I wish I felt like I did yesterday."

However, it can be like yesterday if we realize that whatever is happening right now will pass. We can get through it. The joy and wonderful things will be there again.

For this, we chant. We meditate. We get in touch with our true Self.

30

POTLUCK SPIRITUALITY

IN OUR WORLD today we think, "Hinduism says this, Buddhism says this, Christianity says this, Judaism says this, Islam says this." We say, "It's all one!" We take the various teachings and practices and mix them, and say, "Okay, I know the Truth now. I know it because I'm beyond it all."

We've all had potluck meals. You know how it goes. Somebody brings a bowl of Chinese food. Somebody brings a bowl of Indian food. Somebody else brings a bowl of Italian food. You look at the tray and you can't decide which taste you want to enjoy—the soy sauce or the curry sauce or the tomato sauce. You say, "Oh well, it's potluck so I should live with it."

But if the person coordinating did it properly, he would say, "This one's bringing that, that one's bring that, that other one's bringing that." It would all work together.

The same thing happens in the name of religion. People try to take a little bit of this, a little bit of that, a little bit of something else. And they think, "I got it."

Whatever spiritual tradition, whichever path, you choose, stick with it and follow it. Allow its taste to stay with you.

31

I AM THAT

THE MIND NEEDS something to focus upon, so we use the mantra *So'ham*, or *Haṁsa*. The simple meaning of *So'ham* is "I am That."

Shaivism says *So'ham* is the sound the breath makes when you breathe in and out. The scriptures say it happens 21,600 times a day. If we were able to repeat the mantra that many times, it would be great.

In the beginning, you might use *So'ham* as a way to focus, but as you continue to practice you are able to just listen to the breath making that sound.

Through awareness, we shift from identifying with whatever it is we are identifying with right now to identifying with the Truth, "I am That."

32

THERE IS NOTHING TO BECOME

WE DO SO MANY THINGS these days in our effort to become perfect. We release negativity. We try to become whole. We try to do this or do that. Similarly, we see our spiritual pursuit as something we want to become.

Eventually, we get to a point where all of this—what I call spiritual paraphernalia—doesn't matter. What matters is the state of our mind.

If the mind itself is not at peace, if it has not understood what "I am That" means, then everything else is just an external covering.

When the mind has come to a deep experience of "I am That," you have really understood what meditation is. In that space there is nothing to become. It is a space of joy. You are just happy being who you are. You realize you don't have to do anything to please anybody else. You don't have to do anything to please yourself, either. You can just remain content, still.

When people ask, "What am I supposed to become?" I tell them that in my experience there is nothing to become. If anything, we have to become nothing.

33

THE WHEEL OF COLORS

WHEN WE LOOK at most experiences in life, we see there is pain at the end. Most things we do are pleasurable in the moment or for a period of time. But they bring about pain in the end. At some point, one or another organ in our body is likely to become the cause of pain.

The sages want us to become aware that our attachment to all these transitory things is the source of pain-filled *vikalpas*, movements of the mind.

Through lifetimes, we have been in painful situations, and the patterns repeat themselves. We come to a sage, and he tries to point out how we can become free of these patterns.

I'm sure you have seen one of those big lamps that give the effect of flashing red, green, blue, yellow, white as they rotate. To me, that wheel of colors is like the different vikalpas. It seems as if the lamp itself has changed color, but it hasn't really. The color of its light just changes for a transitory moment as the lamp rotates.

In the same way, Consciousness exists untouched, unchanging. But the vikalpas within us arise and color that Consciousness.

For example, two people fall in love with each other. Ex-husbands and ex-wives always agree with me on this. When you first meet, he or she is the best thing that ever happened in your life.

Five, ten, twenty years later—or even five minutes later—the vikalpa changes from green, filled with love, to red: "Stop! He's the worst thing that could have happened in my life!"

The person is who he is. He has not changed. You have to look within and ask, "What is this vikalpa?"

Yoga teaches us to become aware of this constantly changing pattern of vikalpas. Catch yourself. Don't live on the wheel of colors: Red, green yellow! Red, green yellow! Red, green, yellow!

Sometimes when we play with our vikalpas, depending upon what color another person is in, he or she responds accordingly. If it happens that we both have yellow vikalpas, great! We think, "Perfect! We are in sync!"

But then yellow changes to red or green or blue or black. All of a sudden you say, "How did I ever think I could work with this person?"

Like a yogi, learn to be unaffected by the wheel of colors. Understand that this, too, shall pass. What you feel right now is only a momentary feeling that a vikalpa is creating within you.

34

UPLIFT YOURSELF

WHEN WE FEEL PAIN, we go to whatever we have decided is our temple of God or place of worship, and we sit there. We talk to the unseen. We cry. We laugh.

And that unseen talks back to us. We don't hear physical words through the ears, yet we feel comforted.

Ask yourself, "Who is that who has cradled me? In whose lap have I sat? Who has lifted me from my suffering and pain?"

The *Śrīmad Bhagavad Gītā* says, "One should uplift oneself by oneself."

Whenever you find that something sad or painful is happening, remind yourself to talk to that one you don't see. And the answers will come.

You can get into your car. Open the windows. Open the sun roof. Play loud music. After a few moments, you'll ask yourself, "Why did I do what I did?" Because as long as you don't indulge in a bad feeling, the mind lets it go.

This is what yoga gives us.

Uplift yourself. Each moment, each year, each month—uplift yourself. Don't stay there long. The faster you get out of it, the faster you move along in life.

35

THE SUPERPOWER WITHIN

EVERYBODY THINKS, "I'm going to find a superpower. I'm going to connect to that power, and then my job will be done."

We must realize that the superpower doesn't exist somewhere else. It lies within us.

We always think, "I'll just hold onto his shirt tails and tag along." But yoga is about independence. It's about freedom, about being able to stand on our own feet. It's about finding our own understanding and arriving at our own conclusions.

THE RIVER OF LIFE

EACH HUMAN BEING is born into the river of life.

This river has two banks: the bank with form, and the bank without form. The bank with form is the world with all its various desires, wants, and needs. The formless bank is the divine, is God.

Born into this river of life, we are constantly dragged down by the desires of the world. As long as we are filled with wants and desires, the world has a hold on us. We have many great reasons to say why we are pulled to the other shore of the world.

Tukārām Mahārāj says that wrong actions we performed in a past life come as disease in our next life. We can go to great doctors, but they won't have the power to remove wrong actions committed in a life before.

Only one who has been blessed by God has that power. Therefore, we have to hold the hands of the holy man, the saint, the Guru, who have been blessed by the Lord. Holding the hands of these people, our destiny is purified by the grace of God.

37

WORSHIP OF THE FORM IS
A PATH TO THE FORMLESS

ONE OF THE QUESTIONS that arises in people's minds is "Should I follow the path of idol worship or should I follow the path of the formless, where there is no external worship, as such?"

If we sit to meditate without a form on which to focus the mind, without any object or point of reference, the mind tends to run off in different directions. But if it has a focus, a form to worship, it can become one-pointed.

As we rise above the mind and the thought forms it constantly creates, we can begin to let go of that form.

A plane flies through air, but it needs a runway to take off. In the same way, the various practices we do offer a way by which we can get to the experience of divinity. Then we can dwell in the sky of oneness.

38

LOVE YOUR SELF

IF SOMEBODY TELLS US to "love your Self," that's not always so easy. We can't see the Self. We don't really know what the Self is.

So a form is given to the Self—whether it is Śiva, Rāma, Kṛṣṇa, or one of a myriad other deities.

We feel drawn to this deity, we have affection for it. As devotees, we honor and worship our chosen deity. We perform rituals and ceremonies. As we meditate on our deity, we imbibe the qualities of that being, of the Guru, of God.

Over time, any sense of difference between us and our Beloved dissolves.

39

WHO IS THE GURU?

A VERSE FROM THE *GURU GĪTĀ* says, "I offer my salutations to *Śrī Sadguru*, who is bliss Absolute, always attentive, always at rest, always in the state of freedom. His mind is pure like the sky; always focused on the experience 'I am That.' Knowing that One which is without a second, he is eternal, free of all impurities. He is steady; situated within all of us as the witness of everything that happens; beyond all feelings, thoughts, and emotions; free of the three *guṇas*. To that Sadguru I offer my salutations."

This verse encompasses everything one needs to know and understand about the Guru.

Yet when we live with the Guru, we see a human who looks like us, talks like us, eats like us, wakes up like us, and goes to the bathroom like us. So the mind thinks, "Can he be a saint? I thought a saint didn't do all those things."

The scriptures remind us that a great being only takes a human form, coming to live and work with us, for the sake of the advancement of humanity. Of course, each saint also has his own *prārabdha* karma, the karma allotted to him in this lifetime, that he must go through.

The difference between an ordinary human being and one established in the state of oneness with divinity is that the Guru is a master of his mind, not its slave. The Guru's mind is always focused on divinity, not distracted or disturbed by whatever else is going on around him.

THE GURU LEADS YOU TO TRUTH

BABA DID NOT SIT US DOWN each day and say, "Today I'm going to teach you this technique of meditation" or "I'm going to teach you this way of breathing." We simply lived with him, worked with him, and spent our time around him. If we ever slackened or became a little bit lazy, he would become, seemingly, very angry. And we would learn that way.

There are no books that say, "This is how the Guru will behave." So watch out! The scriptures simply say the Guru will lead you to the experience of Truth.

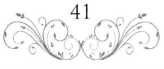

41

BE CONSCIOUS AT ALL TIMES

BABA DIDN'T TEACH US chanting and meditation so we would just sit in one place.

For those who lived with him, from the time you woke up, throughout the day, until the time you slept, and through your sleep, he wanted that the awareness of Consciousness, the understanding of Consciousness, the experience of Consciousness remain.

42

OPEN YOUR EYES

IF YOU WATCH the sunrise, as the sun rises, darkness simply vanishes.

In the moment of that light, you don't think to yourself, "Where is the darkness?" You simply appreciate the light.

In the same way, we each can learn always to be filled with light. When there is light, there is no darkness.

But we sometimes think, "Too much light!" And we close our eyes.

The Guru simply tells us, "Open your eyes." And the light is there.

43

KEEP PEDALLING

AS YOU MEDITATE, the light within will shine more and more brightly.

Take the example of a dynamo on a bicycle. For that light to stay lit, the wheel must keep moving; the dynamo must keep rotating. On its own, it may remain lit for a few moments. But to keep it brightly lit, you must keep pedalling. Of course, the chain must also be connected. Otherwise, you put forth effort, but you don't go anywhere.

44

THE BLUE PEARL

THE SAGES TALK about the subtle bodies, or energy bodies, within us as light. Tukārām Mahārāj said he experienced red, white, black, yellow, and different colors. Depending on a person's inner state, you will see different colors emanate from him or her. Modern people call it an aura.

Baba used to say that whenever he saw somebody approaching him, he first saw light. He didn't see the individual, all he saw was light. For him, that was the light of the Self, which he called the Blue Pearl.

He said that when he was going through his process of meditation, he sometimes saw the Blue Pearl coming and going. As he became established in his experience of meditation, that blue light became steady.

Baba said the Blue Pearl lives within everybody, therefore everybody is good.

So, think good thoughts. Speak good words. Do good deeds. Lead a good life.

Of course, each of us must think about what good means to us. We have to come to the understanding that all the things we do, think, see, hear, eat, and so on feed into each other.

45

THE STATE OF YOUR HEART

IF WE LOVE ourselves and have compassion for ourselves, then hatred cannot exist within us. There is simply kindness. Every thought, every action, every moment is filled with love. No matter what is happening, even if our enemy comes, we simply express love and kindness.

But some people think, "What matters is that others see me as kind and sweet. It's enough that my behavior be loving and generous, that my external form not be malevolent."

But yoga says no, what matters is what is going on within. You can appear to be kind on the surface, but it is the state of your heart that counts. When the heart is immersed in non-violence, you are free to perform actions that are appropriate to the circumstances.

EXPAND YOUR UNIVERSE

THE OTHER DAY someone was trying to walk up the stairs by Shrinivas, and a chipmunk would not move. The person said, "He doesn't move! He won't move!"

I said, "He wants you to move. He wants to sit where he's sitting. He doesn't realize why you think he has to move. He can't understand why you can't go over this way or that way. You stand there and go, 'Move!' and he's like, 'What?'"

Funny, aren't we? We always think it is the other who has to move. We never think it is I who has to move.

Yoga teaches us to constantly learn to weave, to move, to be flexible. Life is beautiful if we are able to stretch, to expand.

We tend to remain contracted within our own universe. We don't want to expand. We think, "Why should I? Let him expand, let her expand." But then the other individual thinks the same.

How do you begin to expand?

I would say the very first thing is to look at what you do every day in life, and do that a bit differently every day.

How? That you have to figure out.

47

SPEND TIME IN YOUR OWN COMPANY

EACH DAY spend time in your own company—devoid of television, devoid of your mobile, devoid of a computer, devoid of everything external. Not even books.

Take fifteen minutes, at least, each day just to be with yourself. Ask yourself, "Where am I? Am I a better person? A better child? A better man, woman?"

Each day, take time and sit with yourself so you will know who you are when you go out into society.

48

HUG YOURSELF

TRY THIS. Go to a mirror, stand in front of it, and hug yourself.

If you've never done it, go do it. Not because you lack anything, but just so you feel what it is to love thyself.

Look at yourself smile. Look at your eyes. Imagine if you could just go out into the world feeling like this.

49

WHY REACT?

AS YOU GO through the process of sādhanā, you begin to become more aware of yourself. What do most humans do? We react. We constantly react, and in our reaction we do not really see the situation.

Yoga teaches us to step back. Because reaction will only cause another reaction. So you stop for a moment; you sit with yourself. Yoga calls this contemplation.

You ask yourself, "Why should I react?"

Somebody calls you a fool, an idiot, stupid. Then he says you're a bigger fool for not reacting. The sages ask, "Do you become a fool because someone says you're a fool?"

No. The other person becomes a greater fool in the very next instant when he does not get the desired reaction from you.

50

YOGA IN THE MARKETPLACE

THE BEST WAY to study yoga is in the midst of people.

You can take the teachings, which are present in your mind, and sit in the midst of a mall or a marketplace, or anywhere nobody knows you. Just observe and watch the interactions of all the various people, most of whom don't know each other.

Then, if you are open enough and willing enough, also interact.

For me, that is easy because I am strange compared with the rest of the world. You could also dress up strangely—or do something else that is unusual—and sit in the marketplace. You will be noticed, and then you can observe what happens.

When King Akbar asked Birbal, "How many people are blind?" Birbal said, "I'll tell you in a week."

He went to the marketplace with his attendant, and sat there sewing.

Of course, everybody in that kingdom knew Birbal was the king's minister, so as they walked by, they would ask, "Birbal, what are you doing?"

He told his attendant, "Write down 'He is blind.'"

When Birbal had not shown up in court after three or four days, the king went to the marketplace. When he saw Birbal sewing, he said, "What are you doing?"

Birbal said, "Write the king's name also."

Seven days later he went back to court. He said, "O King, everybody, including you, is blind."

The king said, "Why?"

"Every single person saw I was sewing, yet everyone asked, 'O Birbal, what are you doing?'"

In the same way, you can go to the marketplace and do something strange. It is a great opportunity to learn about yourself.

You probably thought I would say learn about others. But it is an opportunity to see your own reactions. Not everybody will simply say, "Oh, you are sewing." They may ask, "Why are you sewing?" Or "What are you sewing that for?"

This question will be asked in many different ways. In each moment, you have to become aware of the Self and not react, not be touched by what is happening.

When you can do this, you have understood what Lord Kṛṣṇa says in the *Bhagavad Gītā*: "The Self dwells within this body, yet it is not tainted by what happens in this body."

51

BANANA PEEL

WHEN YOU WALK on the street, suppose you see a banana peel. Now, most of us have probably never stepped on one. But we've seen others do it, so we know what happens when one steps on a banana peel.

The external banana peel we can see. The mental banana peel, not always.

On the outside, we know to step over or avoid it. What sādhanā teaches is the *viveka*, the discrimination, we need to avoid the mental banana peel.

We acquire the wisdom not to fall, always to look up. Even if we do fall or slip, each time we catch ourselves more quickly. Just as we see a banana peel on the outside from a distance, we train ourselves to watch the mental banana peel coming up, too.

When you have conquered the internal banana peel, you have success in life.

52

THE WORLD IS AS YOU SEE IT

THE SAINTS SEE THE WORLD as filled with divinity, with Consciousness. We see the opposite. We try to look for Consciousness, whereas the saints see everything as Consciousness, just as it is.

The *Yoga Vāsiṣṭha* says, "The world is as you see it."

We are all part of that same Consciousness, yet we perceive and see things in our own way. Depending upon our upbringing, our training, our past karmas, we have our own way of looking at life, looking at others, and looking at the world.

When we see the world through our limited ideas, we think somebody is good, somebody is bad, somebody is great, somebody is small. Instead, we want to go beyond all these external differences and see oneness.

Therefore, we must learn to fill our mind with the knowledge of God, with the knowledge of the Absolute. From this viewpoint, we see the world as filled with Consciousness.

53

THE SPIDER'S WEB

THE *UPANIṢADS* give the simple example of a spider's web. We see the intricate web, with its many lines and patterns, but that web was created by a single spider from a single strand. And the spider can also take that strand back into itself.

In the same way, universal Consciousness projects from within itself this multitude of forms we know as the universe—the world, ourselves, all the different lands and oceans and what not.

It may seem as if it comes from many different sources, but just like the spider's web, everything comes from that one universal Consciousness.

It is not easy to comprehend that such diversity could arise from one source. The philosophy of Shaivism says the universe is created by *spanda*. Its sound, *Oṁ*, is vibrating at all times, in everything.

54

RISE TO THE EXPERIENCE
OF "I AM CONSCIOUSNESS"

OFTEN WE THINK of ourselves according to how somebody else tells us we are.

Somebody says, "You're smart." Somebody says, "You're stupid." Somebody says, "You're wise." Somebody says, "You're foolish." Whatever it is, that thought stays with us.

Instead, stop and become aware of yourself. Ask yourself, "Who am I?"

Of course, the highest answer is "I am Consciousness."

You might not get there immediately, but as you slowly rise to the experience of "I am Consciousness," you become established in the levels of "who am I?"

Let nothing and nobody disturb you from that understanding. If anything does disturb you, use that as an opportunity to become more firmly rooted in the true understanding of "who am I?" so nothing on the outside will be able to shake it.

55

WHO AM I?

IN VEDĀNTA, Śrī Ādī Śaṅkarācārya says one should always contemplate these questions: "Who am I? What is this world? What is it all made of? Why am I here? What am I made of? What is all this about?"

When we ask ourselves, "Who am I?" our immediate answer usually is related to the body-mind and its attainments. We think, "I am a doctor, I am a lawyer, I am a musician, I am a swami," or whatever role life has carved out.

The sages tell us that such identifications are false or unreal. They are transitory. When the body is dropped, there is no longer identification with any particular role. So we must keep asking ourselves, "Who am I really?"

Sometimes this process can be scary. Ever since childhood our self-identity has been tied to our body, name, gender, nationality, aptitude, and so on.

Then one day we begin to realize, "I am not who I think I am."

That is when the mind starts contemplating more deeply, "Who am I? What is this life for? What am I doing in this world? Surely there is more than just waking up each morning, drinking coffee, and going to work, then coming home at the end of the day, eating, watching television, and going to sleep."

Think of what animals do. They wake in the morning, drink something, go hunting for food, feed, talk in their animal language, and go to sleep. But we have the good fortune to have received a human body and are able to self-reflect.

It's not just that we have the ability to think, we can actually think about the nature of reality, about the meaning and purpose of life. We can explore the notion of Self, diving deep into the ocean of Consciousness. These capacities differentiate us from animals, but only if we use them.

56

I AM GOD THE WAY I AM

MAY WE OPEN our minds and our hearts and our eyes and expand ourselves. Sādhanā is all about expansion and growth, and not staying with the limited thought "Oh me, poor me."

Have the realization "I am God the way I am, here in this moment." Not "I will become God" or "I have to become God."

It is a matter of accepting ourselves with all our hearts, of knowing "I am who I am."

57

A SUBTLE SHIFT

ALL THE STUDYING, practice, and contemplation we do is in preparation for the subtle shift that will take place within us. The mind constantly contemplates and asks questions.

All this is so we're prepared for the moment when, if the Guru asks, "Who are you?" there is no answer.

58

THAT WHICH MAKES POSSIBLE

THE ROOT OF THE WORD *sādhanā* means that which makes possible, the means, the way.

As long as you think, "I must do it," sādhanā remains separate from you. But when you realize, "It is part of me, part of my life, and something I enjoy," it becomes easy.

As faith and devotion develop, sādhanā starts to bear fruit.

59

DEVOTION AND SERVICE

BHAKTI, DEVOTION, AND *SEVĀ*, selfless service, go hand in hand. You cannot understand sevā until you have bhakti. And you cannot have bhakti unless you have the attitude of sevā.

Both have a quality in common: humility.

Many people have an issue with this. They think, "If I am performing actions, why should I not look at the fruits?"

We must understand how the sages see this. In the *Bhagavad Gītā*, Lord Kṛṣṇa asks, "Who are you to think 'I' am performing actions?"

When it comes to bhakti and sevā, the very first thing to eliminate is the "I" that will have bhakti, the "I" that will do sevā. Until that happens, there is no bhakti, there is no sevā. There is just an "I" thinking it is doing the act of bhakti, an "I" thinking it is doing the act of sevā.

If you watch people who really have bhakti and do sevā—who have eliminated the "I"—you will see they're always in a good mood.

You might ask, "Why do you always feel good? Why are you always singing, humming away?"

They will say, "Because all I know is to worship my Lord. All I know is to sing to my Lord. I know nothing else."

Don't think the Lord is only some deity. The Lord can be the wife or the husband, also. Everybody can be happy with each other.

60

OFFER YOUR SERVICE
IN THE WORLD

INCORPORATE YOUR SPIRITUAL PRACTICE into your mundane world. As you do your job, have the attitude that those tasks are also sevā. By doing them, you are furthering your sādhanā.

All the things you do to make money, to feed your family, are part of your spiritual experience.

Carry a japa mālā or maybe keep a little picture so the mind is reminded of the presence of God, the presence of the Guru.

When the mind gets tense, put your hand into your pocket. Instead of finding a pack of cigarettes, find your mālā. As you repeat the mantra, the mind becomes calm.

If you are in your own cubicle or your own office, stop and breathe deeply. Reconnect with your Self. Then you can naturally let go of whatever frustration has developed.

61

SAVE YOURSELF FIRST

SOMETIMES WE GET CAUGHT in the idea "I need to save the world."

The sages say, "Save yourself. Help yourself."

If we save ourselves, if the light within us is kindled, if we become a flaming torch, we can be a beacon in the darkness. But if we are in the darkness ourselves, what is the point of going around saying, "Let me tell you what ignorance is"?

Therefore, the *Upaniṣads* say, "Wake up first, understand the Truth, and then automatically you can share it with others."

If all of us are in a hole and we all want to get out, one of us has to get out first and give a hand to pull the others out.

In the same way, when we see the light within and understand what the Self is, it's not an intellectual notion. It is a direct experience. Then without saying anything, without doing anything, we bring that light to others.

62

LEARN FROM THE SUN

IMAGINE IF THE SUN were to think every morning, "Should I rise or should I not rise?"

Such a question could not arise. The sun does its duty always. It doesn't think to itself, "This person is good, this person is bad." It sheds its light. It gives us fire, warmth.

We must learn from all these things that exist in nature—the sun, the trees, the rain. They all give, and whoever wants to take from them can do so.

In the same way, when we experience divinity, love, within ourselves, we don't have to ask, "How much will I give to myself? How much will I give to others?"

When we connect with the reservoir of love within us, it is boundless.

63

BE BIG

IN ANCIENT INDIA, the eldest female always ate last. She was the Lakṣmī, the goddess of abundance, of the household. That is how she served and offered her love. Each individual in the family was loved by that mother.

Of course, today we think everybody should sit together, but you can imagine how big that heart had to be to always love everybody, to feed everybody, to take care of everybody.

We have to learn to be big.

Often people say, "That person is mean. We should be mean back to him."

I say, "God, meditation—all that comes afterwards. First just love people. When you meet them, let them feel welcomed. Treat them as they have never been treated."

Of course, it's difficult. You think, "Why should I be nice to them? They are not nice."

You have to ask yourself, "Why aren't they nice?" Perhaps they are coming from a place of defending themselves. If you can love them, if you can be kind to them, you create a small opening.

64

KINDNESS AND DETACHMENT

WHEN YOU READ STORIES about the great beings, you understand that kindness, compassion, and love are given, yet they are given with detachment.

You come to understand "I am an individual and that person is an individual, but we both have our own space, our own karma. What I feel and experience in this moment is not necessarily what that individual across from me is going to feel and experience. I am not going to force how I feel upon that individual."

Usually we want the other person to soften up, to see all the compassion we experience. Therefore attachment comes in: "Why don't you feel my kindness? Why don't you feel my love? Why don't you feel my compassion?"

Detachment must be there. We give kindness, we give compassion, we give whatever we want to give. But we must be detached about how another person receives it.

A tree gives it shade, irrespective of the fact that a person is sitting under it. The person may be just resting, gathering his energy to cut down that tree in the next moment. The tree doesn't say, "He's going to cut me down, so I'm going to let my leaves whither away so he doesn't get shade."

A tree just sits, gives shade, and in the next moment that person cuts it down. Great beings live in the same way. They share, they give, and they do not expect anything back.

65

PLEASE THE WORSHIPPER

WE OFFER LIGHT, we offer incense, we offer fruit, we offer food—we offer all these things to the deity we love.

People often ask, "Do you think God will be pleased if I do this? Will the Guru be pleased?"

We have to realize, as it says in the *Guru Gītā*, *Brahmānandam parama sukhadam*. "God exists in bliss at all times." The Guru lives in bliss at all times, constantly content.

So will my worship please God or will it please me, the worshipper?

The answer is it pleases the worshipper. It is we who experience the joy. When we offer devotion with great humility, with great love, the fruit of that is that we experience great love. The external things we offer are simply a token of the devotion we feel in our heart.

66

FIRST OFFER YOUR FOOD

THE *UPANIṢADS* TELL US to be careful how we handle food, how we think of food, and how we consume food. Our tradition is that food must be consumed sitting down, after we have washed our hands.

First food is offered to the Lord. According to the scriptures, food that hasn't been offered to God has no conscious value.

The next time you pull into a drive-thru, think for a moment. What are you going to put inside your body? How will it make you feel?

We have anger, we have frustration. The sages say that the food we put inside ourselves is what creates those thoughts, those emotions.

As we offer our food, we sing a mantra from the fourth chapter of the *Bhagavad Gītā*. It says that Brahman is the enjoyer as well as the one to whom the food is offered. In other words, the food is God, it is offered to God, and it is enjoyed by God.

With this understanding, we must enjoy not only food but everything in life, after offering it to God.

67

THE SUBTLE ESSENCE OF FOOD

BABA ALWAYS EMPHASIZED that as people prepare food, instead of gossiping, which is the normal tendency, they should chant the mantra.

Because the vibration you put into the food is what you take from that food when you eat it. The subtle essence is what ultimately remains because the gross part of the food is gotten rid of by the body.

Therefore, people who cook must put good energy into the food so that others may be uplifted.

68

BECOME STRONG

WHEN WE GET SICK, we think it's due to a virus, a bacteria, or some influence from the outside. But yoga sees it as a symptom of what is going on inside of us.

Because of what is going on within, the mind becomes weak.

As the mind becomes weak, the body becomes weak. When the body is weak, it becomes susceptible to viruses or germs or whatever can cause sickness.

So yoga teaches us to strengthen the mind, strengthen ourselves, and thus be able to withstand any onslaught from the outside.

69

BE CLEAR ABOUT YOUR GOAL

OFTEN WE ASK OURSELVES, "Why does it seem like I put forth effort but I don't arrive at my destination?"

First of all, Vedānta would say you have to become clear about the destination, about your goal: "Where am I am going?" You must be aware and remain focused upon the goal.

Second, figure out how you are going to get from where you are now to your destination. What are the pitfalls? What are the drawbacks? What are the different ways to get from where you are now to your destination?

If you're not clear about these two things—What is my goal? What is my path?—most of your time will be spent floundering.

You might say, "But the goal is always changing."

The goal is not always changing. On the spiritual path, the goal is always the same. It is your desire that constantly fluctuates.

So create a plan for your life. What destiny, the planets and other people have to say are all external factors. Clarity has to arise in your mind.

70

CREATE A SCHEDULE

I SUGGEST that anyone who follows the path of yoga create a daily schedule. Try to follow it every single day.

The mind loves discipline. If you think people don't like discipline, I would say that's not true. You give a child discipline, and he does very well. Because he knows exactly what is expected of him.

We're just older children. We also need a discipline. As we give ourselves discipline, we see that it works.

A REGULAR PRACTICE

CHANTING BRINGS ME to a space of joy, of ecstasy. Some people love to repeat the mantra. Others like to become focused on their breath. For others, just sitting still brings them to the space of quietude.

No matter what path or practice you like, do it regularly for some time. Make the time for it, as you make time for other things, and do it.

As you allow it to become a regular practice or habit, you will find that transformation gradually takes place.

You don't have to constantly say to yourself, "I want to be transformed" or "I want to become God" or "I want to become perfect." Just follow that small practice.

It might be simply lighting a candle for a few minutes and becoming aware of your inner divinity. Whatever it is, do it. It can be in the morning, afternoon, evening, or before going to bed.

In this way, allow yourself to live in remembrance of Truth, of God. As that remembrance increasingly stays with you, it will create the transformation you seek.

CONTENTMENT

SOMETIMES YOU HAVE a glimpse of contentment during your practice and you pray and ask, "How can I have more?"

Think about why you had that experience of contentment.

It is because in that moment your mind was still. You weren't thinking. You weren't worrying. You just allowed yourself to be. You allowed everything to be.

Try this. Every morning watch what happens when you first awaken, before any thoughts come into the mind.

In the state of sleep, the mind is quiet and you're cut off from dealings with the world, so you come close to the Consciousness that exists within the body. When you awaken, you find the experience of contentment is still there. It may last only a few seconds, but if you pay attention to it, you will feel it.

Try to hold that state as you go about performing your activities of daily life. It's not easy, but if you keep at it, it will happen.

TAKE OFF THE BLINDERS

YOGA IS ABOUT removing our blinders. We become free of all concepts, of all thoughts that arise in the mind.

Baba talked about the blinders they put on horses that draw the carriages or tongas in India. This is done so the horse does not see what is to its left or right, but only sees what is ahead. He said that in sādhanā it is great to be one-pointed, to know where you are going, and to look nowhere else but at your goal. At the same time, sādhanā removes those blinders so your vision expands to include what is behind, what is ahead, and what is on both sides.

The *Upaniṣads* talk about God being above, below, to your left, to your right, in front and behind.

When I first read this many years ago, I thought, "What do they mean? Of course God is everywhere." Yet we tend to think God is only in the Guru's picture, in the holy items we worship. We never think God could be in the bathroom. Or that God could be the garbage collector.

But the scriptures ask us to take off our blinders and contemplate, "In what place or moment or time does God not exist?"

CONSTANT REMEMBRANCE
OF THE DIVINE

BABA GAVE US some very simple practices to perform. Get up each morning, do your chanting, do your meditation, and then go about your life. Come back at the end of the day after having bathed, meditate, and then go to bed.

Each day begins and ends with devotion to God. Thus, it is filled with constant remembrance of the divine.

In most temples in India, *āratī*, the waving of lights, is performed three times a day. We of course think it is so the deity will be pleased. But it is really for the benefit of the individual who performs the worship.

In the early days, everybody lived in a village. Each village had a temple, a place of God. In the morning, before he went to work, a person would visit the priest or holy person there and spend a few moments in worship. At midday, the person would pass by the temple and spend a few more moments. And again in the evening, on his way back from work, he'd go and sit in the temple.

We might say, "How boring. Those villagers didn't have television. They didn't have mobile phones. They didn't have the Internet. They didn't even have cars."

They may not have had all of the things we have today, but they were content, they were happy, they were satisfied.

75

CONSISTENCY BEARS FRUIT

WE HAVE A KUMQUAT TREE HERE. Suppose the owners wanted to change houses every few months, and they thought this tree should be in the backyard of each new house. So they took it with them. Some of the time it would be in Melbourne, some of the time it would be in Canberra, some of the time it would be in Sydney.

Think what would happen to the tree after a couple of moves. It would die because it didn't like the soil in one place, or it didn't like the weather conditions in another. Most of all, it would be in shock at constantly being moved about.

In the same way, if you don't give your mind a constant practice, something to hold onto year after year after year, and if you don't give it a focus, it never becomes steady.

Find a practice that works for you and follow it diligently. As you offer yourself in a committed fashion, the mind slowly gets used to that sādhanā, to the daily continuous effort you put forth. Then you begin to see the fruit consistency bears for you.

HAVE PASSION FOR
YOUR PRACTICE

THE SAGES TELL US to have love, to have passion, for spiritual practice.

Of course, there are days we don't feel like doing our practice. Whether it is meditating or chanting or whatever practice, we have so many excuses why we can't do it.

On those days especially, force yourself to do it.

Even though you feel, "I don't want to be doing this now," make yourself do it. You will break through a barrier, a wall, within yourself. As you break through that, what arises is the feeling of ecstasy, of joy.

You realize, "I'm not doing it for anybody else. I'm doing it for my own pleasure."

EFFORT AND GRACE

YOGA TEACHES US about two things: effort and grace.

Effort is put forth by the individual. Grace is provided by the divinity that dwells within us.

Of course, the mind always thinks, "I'm putting forth effort. Where is the grace?"

But it's the opposite. Grace is always present. It is the human who fails to put forth his or her effort.

GRACE IS ALWAYS THERE

IF GRACE IS ALWAYS THERE, and the scriptures tell us the experience of divinity is easy to attain, why when we close our eyes are we not able to see it? As soon as we close our eyes, all we see is thoughts, thoughts, thoughts. And we wonder, "What do I do with my thoughts?"

Thoughts are like little children. When a child cries, "Daddy! Mommy!" and nags and nags about something, you finally think, "Let me just do what he wants and he'll be happy."

You do it for a few minutes, and he's happy.

But then he comes back. "It broke!" Or my brother broke it!"

This is how thoughts are. We follow one thought because we think "If I just work out this one, I'll be free." But as soon as that thought is over, another comes up. And we think, "Well, just this one…" This is how it goes.

At some point, we ask ourselves, "How did I get myself into all this? Who is to blame? Who is responsible?" Of course, we don't think we did any of it. But if you stop and think about it, we created it ourselves. And we keep it going.

One day Sheikh Nasruddin needs to borrow a wagon. So he gets up and goes to his friend's house. On the way, he starts to think, "What if he doesn't want to give me the wagon? What if he tells me it is not there? What if he doesn't like me anymore?"

As he is walking, his mind has all these thoughts. When he arrives at his friend's house, he knocks on the door and says, "I don't want your wagon. Keep it. I'm not even interested in it." And he turns around and goes home.

Like this, the mind creates and creates and creates. And we sustain and sustain and sustain it. And the cycle goes on.

The purpose of yoga, of meditation, is to finally catch ourselves from that process of creation and sustenance and allow it to dissolve. Simply tell yourself, "I need the wagon. I'm going to get it. If it's there, fine; if it's not there, fine." Then the grace that is always present can be easily experienced.

GOD INSURANCE

WE LIVE UNDER the guarantees of life insurance, health insurance, legal insurance, and I don't know what other forms of insurance. "I'm protected. I am taken care of!" we think. "I am safe because one of the insurances will kick in when I need it."

This is how we as human beings try to protect ourselves. Though we can't stop a calamity from happening, somehow we feel secure because everything is insured.

Nevertheless, if nature decides it is time for this individual soul to move on, it will make sure we are in the right place, at the right time, for that to take place.

For this reason, Baba used to say, "The only insurance you need is God insurance."

Of course, that is the one insurance policy we likely don't have. What we need is a greater policy, the insurance of God, that covers us in every way at all times.

The only premium you have to pay for it is *śraddhā*, faith. Just as you pay your premiums regularly to make sure an insurance policy continues, you offer your devotion and your prayers regularly to God. In return, you have the assurance that God will always be with you.

WORTHINESS

WHEN A SAGE uses the microscopic eye of his mind to look at the worthiness of a person, he doesn't look at the person's beauty. He doesn't look at the person's wealth. He doesn't look at the social status of that person. The sage looks at whether this person has the ability to carry that which the sage has to give.

A person is worthy who, having received initiation, never deviates from the practice, from the teaching, from that which has been given to him or her.

81

SPIRITUAL EGO

YOU MAY THINK, "That person is so horrible! All he does is smoke, drink, and go out and have fun. He never thinks of God."

The truth is, if such a person remembers God even once, God is happy. Because God in His compassion thinks, "At least he thought of me once in the midst of all his sense pleasures."

Whereas you may consider yourself to be so pure. You talk about God all the time, more than anyone you know. Yet, no matter how many times you think of God, it's never enough.

Now, don't say, "Let me get involved in some sense pleasures because then I only have to think of God once." Don't trick yourself!

You have elevated yourself to your present state and you can only go higher and higher. The more time you spend with your mind totally engrossed in the divine, the closer you will come to God.

As you go about your daily tasks, keep repeating the mantra—not just singing it in the back of your head, but always remaining aware of it.

82

TWO TYPES OF SEEKERS

AS I TRAVEL the world, I meet two kinds of seekers.

One kind performs daily sādhanā, but when he comes across some difficulty or obstacle, he stops his practices, thinking, "I must first resolve this issue, then I can continue."

The second type also has obstacles and issues, but he continues on with his practices while trying to resolve the issue.

See the difference?

Imagine, a person stops in the middle of the highway and looks at the map and says, "Until I know which direction I'm going, I am not going to move." Meanwhile, the cars behind are honking and bumping.

He realizes, "I must keep moving while I figure out where I am going."

In this way, grace propels the person in the right direction. Because the person is moving, he is able to resolve any issues that arise in life. But if the person does not move, he doesn't get anywhere and eventually has to be jump-started.

83

BEYOND THE MIND

A SUFI MASTER once said that three kinds of people are the most difficult to teach: those who are delighted they have achieved something; those who, after learning something, are depressed they didn't know it before; and those who are so anxious to progress that they cease to be sensitive to their progress.

You have to ask yourself, "Which one am I?"

Don't feel frustrated that you don't understand. Don't think, "I need to know better than anyone else." Sādhanā is more a matter of the heart than of the mind.

The sages tell us the mind has the ability to think because of the existence of divinity. The divine is what propels the mind to think. Therefore, we can't tell ourselves that we will try to understand the principle of divinity through the mind.

At some point in our seeking, we must go beyond our own mind.

When we come to that place beyond the mind, we become still and quiet. In that place of stillness, we experience divinity. So as seekers, we must first of all become honest with ourselves. Any games we play, we play with ourselves.

84

REMAIN IN THE AWARENESS

IN THE BEGINNING, a seeker thinks there is so much to do to experience oneness with God. But as one progresses on the path, one realizes all that needs to be done is to hold the awareness of unity.

Whatever we do, we must always remain in this awareness. If we hold this awareness, we have it. We've got it. We have truly given our life to God. Then we are in alignment with what universal Consciousness wants.

85

A BIG SHIP DOES NOT
SHAKE IN THE WIND

MANY PEOPLE ARE VERY SERIOUSLY into their practices. But then they slacken a bit. They get involved in what we call the play of the mind. Eventually they catch themselves and once again bring themselves back into alignment with the practices.

This goes on until they come to the understanding that it's okay, this is what is happening. Or they become so strong in their practices that no matter what comes their way, they are not deterred. It doesn't rock them.

This is what you have to work on. It's not a matter of whether you should be spiritual or not be spiritual, whether you are good or bad. It's about becoming solid in your belief of who you are.

A little boat always shakes with some wind. But a big ship does not.

You have to become like the big ship. If you're not so sure who you are or who you should be, there will always be a battle between your ego and your higher Self.

Give up your notions about what is bad and what is good. Some days you love to chant and some days you want to sit quietly. Some days you don't want to meditate or do japa or do anything, you just want to sit. That's okay. The most important thing is doing the practice; the form it takes doesn't matter.

Your awareness of the divine is what is most important.

86

CREATE STILLNESS

CREATE SOME QUIET SPACE in your home. You will see that the stillness you create on the outside begins to fill your mind. Slowly that stillness will permeate your entire being.

THE FRUIT OF SĀDHANĀ

YOU CAN TELL how people are doing in their sādhanā by noticing how they walk, how they speak, how they behave, how they carry themselves.

It's wonderful to light a lamp, to burn incense, to do the various rituals. It shows how religious you are. But until all of this becomes part of you, until you are living it, it means nothing.

When you wave the light with feeling, when you sing to God with feeling, your eyes become filled with tears. When your heart wells up with love, when your whole being is pulsating with joy, know that what you are doing is bearing fruit.

REALIZATION HAPPENS
STEP BY STEP

REALIZATION IS NOT AN EVENT where you wake up one morning and go, "Wow, I'm realized now!" It is a step-by-step process. Revelations and realizations happen continuously.

Yet regardless of where you are in this process and what you might think you are, know that you are God.

DON'T BE IGNORANT,
DON'T BE ENLIGHTENED

ENLIGHTENMENT IS A PROCESS. Of course, we seek instant enlightenment. And we can say enlightenment is instant because understanding can happen in a flash. But first we must take the steps. We must make the effort.

I don't like to say too much about it. Because either you know it or you don't know it. If you don't know it, that's the best state because you can allow yourself to be who you are, without feeling the need to become something. When you know it, that's also the case.

It's the in between stage that is dangerous. You are trying to become something, but you get frustrated because you haven't yet become what you think you should become. Then you go into a state of ignorance in which you think, "This is a little bit better."

But this state of ignorance is even more confusing. So you try to get into a state of total enlightenment. Yet when you get to that so-called total enlightenment, you realize, "Well, actually I'm not enlightened at all."

So the best thing is to just be. Don't be ignorant, don't be enlightened. Allow yourself to be who you are, enjoying what is unfolding in your life in each moment.

QUESTION AND WONDER

IT'S OKAY to question and wonder.

I have seen that people who question and wonder become the staunchest devotees of God because they work through whatever limitations their minds have imposed. They are able to open themselves wider and accept God in all His myriad forms.

A BIGGER UMBRELLA

AS YOU PRACTICE YOGA, miracles can happen. But the sages warn us not to focus on this because it is not what yoga is about.

In India there is a tradition that one always goes to a saint. One says, "Give me blessings. I want a child." When a child is born, that child is brought to the saint. "Give me blessings so he becomes a good boy." And then it is "Give him blessings so he gets a good wife. Give him blessings so he has good children. Give him blessings for a good job."

The saint always says, "Very good, very good."

At some point we have to ask ourselves, "Am I going to continue like this or am I going to seek something greater—a bigger umbrella that covers all these little things?"

We think, "I'm going to take care of this little issue that has been gnawing at me. In meditation today I'll ask God to give me the answer to this problem." We presume that if we take care of this one issue, our life will flow smoothly.

But if we simply meditate without focusing on that issue or making it into a problem, it will dissolve on its own.

ILLUMINATION WILL COME

YOGA TEACHES us that if we have an issue, we should think about it, write about it, and let it simmer. Let it simply be there. It doesn't need to talked about, discussed, or brought up again and again.

If you try this, you will see how Consciousness, in its own way, will one day give you the answer. It may not necessarily be in the next moment. It could even be five, ten, twenty years down the road. But you have to have patience. Illumination will come in its own time.

So many different things need to fall into place for that illumination to happen.

Suppose you want to publish a book. So you type it up and say, "Book ready!" But it still has to go to the editor and the designer. It needs to get laid out, and you need to choose the pictures. Only then does it go to the printer, and you get a proof. If that looks okay, finally the book goes to print.

In life, too, we think, "I want this situation resolved now!" But we must think about how we got into that situation. We have done all these things, and in doing them, he was involved, she was involved, and so on. Now we want all of them to come together at the Thanksgiving table.

But he's not ready. She's sort of ready. That other one is willing to sit at the table if he doesn't come. And you think, "I want this resolved now!" Just as there are many vikalpas within you, many more vikalpas are going on in others, also.

What does the sage do? He sits, not worried about this or that. He simply is still. He does not allow his mind to get affected by all the various vikalpas everybody else has.

FIRST BECOME A FISH

SOMETIMES PEOPLE ASKED BABA, "What will I do when I'm realized, when I know the Self? It will be boring."

He would always say, "First go and realize the Self, then come back and we'll talk about it."

Having been on the path and having pursued the practices, we know it takes energy, time, effort, focus, and awareness to come to the experience of "I am Consciousness, I am Truth." Nevertheless as we continue, the mind slowly begins to shift, to change the way it perceives and experiences things. We look at life in a much broader way.

Tukārām Mahārāj said, "To understand how a fish lives, sleeps, and eats while living in water, you must first become a fish."

In the same way, to be able to say how a sage lives in the experience of Consciousness, you must come to be in that experience yourself. As you live in that experience, you can say what it is and isn't.

Often, however, having become still, we lose ourselves in the experience of oneness, of divinity. Then there is nothing more to be said.

Questions arise as long as you try to experience oneness through the mind. But if you allow yourself to go within and merge with Consciousness, you have no more questions. The experience is everything, so there is nothing else to ask.

94

KEEP MOVING

WHEN PEOPLE COME TO ME and say, "I have all these questions, and you have to help me get moving," I usually say, "Well, get moving first, and as you do, these issues will become clear."

This is the nature of the mind. We place such importance on our issues. We burden ourselves with them. But what does a sage do? He tells us, "This is not an issue. Let go. Move forward."

When Baba was giving *darśan*, however few or many people came, he would always say, "Keep moving, keep moving."

Sometimes I would think, "He knows from previous nights that it is going to end in twenty minutes, so why this constant pressure to keep moving?"

But as I think about it now, I realize it had nothing to do with the darśan line. It was about his teaching to keep moving. Don't stop. Don't get stuck. Don't slow down. Keep moving forward.

As that movement happens, we receive the answers to all our questions.

A CONSTANT LIVING PRACTICE

WHEN THE RELATIONSHIP between a Guru and disciple becomes true, they don't remain as two separate individuals. They become one. Truly speaking, when you become one with that being, or that being becomes one with you, there cannot be a relationship. Because there is just one.

Kabīr says in one of his poems that the path of love is very narrow. Either God walks or I walk. Both cannot tread on this path.

But we always want to be on the safe side. We want to be there, just in case.

The first and most important thing to do in any situation in life is surrender. We must have total surrender, total faith, total trust. There is no question that this is what has to be. Of course, we think we have surrendered, yet we always have a "but."

I want you to bear in mind that the relationship we all have with each other is not as social friends, not as two human beings who know each other. As long as you relate to each other in that way, there will not be growth in sādhanā. You will still be relating at the level of mind.

You have to rise above and realize that what exists is special, is different. What binds us together is the *śakti*, the universal energy.

Therefore, let's not make our relationships such that they are dependent on just the external. Let them become much greater than that.

Be honest and truthful with each other. Because we want to lead a life that is spiritual. For example, if you live with a dichotomy between "this is my life" and "this is my yoga," it won't work. These have to become one. How you live, what you breathe, what you eat, and what you do are all yoga. It has to be a constant, living practice.

SURRENDER

WHEN YOU FLY against the wind in an airplane, it takes longer to get to your destination. When you fly with the wind, you get there faster.

In the same way, in life when we go against the will of the śakti, we find ourselves struggling with it, fighting against it. But when we go with it, everything moves smoothly.

When we surrender to that universal energy, it lets us glide. Because we have aligned ourselves with God.

We don't think of ourselves as separate from God, but one with Him. When we have that understanding, we perceive the world as filled with God.

What is the nature of that surrender? It is not of the body, it is not a physical thing. It is the surrender of the mind and ego, of pride and power. It is a subtle shift within us. This shift is what we are trying to attain, and it can happen in the blink of an eye.

LET GO OF YOUR CUP

WE ALL WISH to experience *parama prema*, supreme love.

Seeking the experience of supreme love, we each come carrying our own cup. We say to the Guru, "Fill this cup."

The Guru says, "Let go of the cup."

We say, "No, no. I've come with this cup. I want you to fill it. How can I let go of it?"

So we spend the next many years doing sādhanā to understand why we must let go of that cup.

98

NECTAR OF DEVOTION

WHEN YOU PUT YOUR HAND in water, either it's wet or it's wet. There are no two ways about it. It's not dry.

In the same way, when we immerse ourselves in devotion, in the love of God, nothing else is important. Nothing else is significant.

Having tasted the nectar of devotion, the nectar of satsaṅg, knowing the ecstasy of singing the name of God, everything else we do in life is simply to pass time.

INDIVIDUAL AND
GROUP PRACTICE

WE HAVE TWO FORMS OF PRACTICE: one is individual, and the other is group.

The individual practice we do by ourselves is tested when we come for a group practice.

You can act at home as if you are a really good meditator. Nobody sees if you get up in five minutes. But then you come and sit with other *sādhakas*, with your peers. You have to sit for an hour and you find yourself fidgeting and thinking, "When is this finished?" You realize you are just fooling yourself at home.

KEEP GOOD COMPANY

YOGA TEACHES that both positive and negative, good and bad, exist within a human. It is a habit among humans to always look at the negative, to look at what is wrong.

So we have satsaṅg—we are in the company of the Truth, in the company of the divine. When we hold the awareness of *sat*, of Truth, satsaṅg becomes a continuous process, fostered when we come together.

Why keep good company? Because depending on the company we keep, we develop the tendencies and habits and qualities of that company.

For a yogi, this does not mean only external good company, but good inner company, as well. Don't deny the existence of the negative, of what some call the dark force, but become more aware of the good.

Good company begins with self. Because I am my first companion. My mind is with me at all times, so my mind always has to be good. If my mind is a good companion, I will always seek good company.

101

KEEP ONLY WHAT IS TRUE

MANY PEOPLE ARE IN THE HABIT of gathering information and trying to put it into mental compartments.

If they're into meditation, they want to know which *chakra* is open and which is closed. They want to know how many years of ignorance have been removed and how many remain.

Like this, as we slowly become free, it is easy to pick up and become addicted to new things.

Eventually, we must learn to keep only that which gives us true contentment, true satisfaction, true happiness.

HOLD YOUR UMBRELLA UP

THE PATH IS ABOUT BECOMING FREE, about experiencing who we really and truly are and getting rid of all the other stuff we collect.

If we hold an umbrella the right way up, all the rain water runs off. Nothing remains. But if we hold the umbrella upside down, the water collects inside.

The normal tendency is to keep the mind upside down. This way, many things are collected, and the mind becomes burdened with so much baggage.

Yoga shows us how turn the mind the right way around. Then what we have collected over the years can fall away. No matter what comes to us, life flows on.

103

TRUE RENUNCIATION

THE YOGA SCRIPTURES tell us to renounce. If we want to be happy, we must renounce; if we want to be at peace, we must renounce.

You ask yourself, "What should I renounce?"

You think perhaps your computer, your television, your friends, your family, or maybe other things to which you're attached.

But those things give you information you use daily. And the people you know are going to stick around. Even the things you have accumulated will stay with you for a while.

When we understand the true meaning of renunciation, we realize what we must renounce are the attachments we have created to whatever we think we cannot live without.

Attachment is what causes pain, suffering, and strife in our life.

Most human beings get up each morning and follow a routine, whether it is coffee, juice, cigarette, walk, or exercise. If for one reason or another, that which they think is needed to start the day does not happen, they don't automatically go on to the next thing. They brood over what didn't occur. And if things don't go well later, they say, "Because I didn't do that first thing, my whole day was shot!"

So in that moment—be it 5:00 am or 6:00 am or 7:00 am—when that first action is not achieved, renounce your attachment to the fact that you did not achieve it today. Automatically go on to action number two. This is true renunciation.

CHANGE

THE REAL EFFECT of contemplation and meditation is change—change in your way of thinking, change in how you act, change in how you react to people.

If none of this is happening, you need to take a good look at your practices of contemplation and meditation.

Sometimes people hold the thought "I want to change," yet they don't change.

It is like putting your foot on the brake and revving the accelerator at the same time, and saying, "I wonder why the car doesn't go anywhere."

Of course the car is not going anywhere. In the same way, you may think you want to change, but unless you do meditation and contemplation with your foot off the brake, it's just a nice thought.

105

BECOME SUBTLE

BABA SAID, "Every day let your meditation grow subtler."

Does that mean you have to sit and just become subtle within yourself? No. That means every action you perform, everything you do, everything that happens through you, must be subtle.

If the mind takes this at a shallow level, we think, "What has the Guru given me? What has this practice given me?"

The questions we must ask ourselves are "How much have I imbibed? How much have I truly taken in? How much does every cell in my body vibrate with that teaching?"

STEPPING STONES

WHEN YOU PLANT A SEED, it doesn't germinate overnight. You take care of it, it grows slowly, and eventually you have a tree.

A child is born, and over a period of time he becomes an adult.

In the same way, the path of yoga is a process of evolution.

Of course, whatever understanding we have gained from practices done over lifetimes comes with us.

Unbeknownst to us, we all begin at different levels. Each of us has our own process we go through. That doesn't mean one is better than the other. You can't get depressed because you are starting at sixty and those other people started at twenty. In the eyes of God, it's all the same.

Yoga gives us stepping stones. Great beings, each in their own way, share with us the different steps on their path. And we, according to our strengths, follow after them and allow ourselves to rise.

ALWAYS MOVE FORWARD

THE EXPERIENCE we attain within is carried from life to life. It certainly will stay with us in this life.

Therefore, we have to remember that we're always going forward. We never go backwards.

The great thing about spiritual evolution is that nothing is repeated over and over and over, unless we create a cycle for ourselves in which we fall again and again and again. But even so, we have a chance to wake up and realize we can avoid those pitfalls. We can learn to catch ourselves.

This is what meditation does for us.

PEARLS OF WISDOM

WE HAVE A CHOICE when it comes to the knowledge we receive.

Imagine a hot piece of metal, a hot iron. If you pour water over it, the water becomes steam and evaporates. On the other hand, an oyster takes a drop of water, and over time makes a pearl out of it.

So we have a choice. We can be hot and excited, and let the knowledge we receive simply evaporate. Nothing goes in. We don't remember anything, don't register anything. Therefore, none of it is used in our life.

Or we can be like the oyster. We can take in those drops, and over time they become pearls of wisdom in our life.

GLOSSARY

ācārya: revered teacher

Ādī Śaṅkarācārya: [788–820] philosopher of Vedānta

Akbar: [1542-1605] Moghul emperor of India

āratī: waving of lights to worship a deity

ātman: the soul

avadhūt: one who has gone beyond body consciousness

Baba Muktānanda: Guru of Swami Nityānanda

bhakti: devotion

Bhagavān Nityānanda: Guru of Baba Muktānanda

Bhagavad Gītā: Hindu scripture

Birbal: King Akbar's prime minister

Brahman: the Absolute

Brahmānandaṁ: the bliss of Brahman

chakra: energy center in the subtle body

darśan: vision of the divine, experienced in the presence of
    a holy being

dharma: righteous law

dṛṣṭi: vision

guṇas: three qualities of nature

Guru Gītā: commentary on the Guru

Guru Pūrṇimā: holiday dedicated to the Guru

Haṁsa: natural mantra; literally, "I am That" [see *So'ham*]

japa: repetition of a mantra

Kabīr: [1440–1518] poet-saint and weaver

karma: law of cause and effect

Kṛṣṇa: Hindu deity, Guru of Arjuna in the *Bhagavad Gītā*

Lakṣmī: Goddess of abundance
Mahāmandaleśvar: a distinguished teacher in the
    Śaṅkarācārya order of monks
mahāsamādhi: final merging with the Absolute
Maitreyī: wife of Yājñāvalkya
mālā: a string of beads used like a rosary
mandir: temple
manaḥprasādaḥ: cheerfulness of mind
mantra: sacred words or syllables
Oṁ: the primordial syllable
parama: supreme
prāṇāyāma: control of the breath
prārabdha: carried over from another life (referring to
karma)
pratyāhāra: withdrawal of the senses
prema: love
Rāma: incarnation of Lord Viṣṇu
sādhaka: seeker
sādhanā: spiritual practices
śakti: the creative energy of the universe; the awakened
    spiritual energy
samādhi: union with the Absolute
sanātana: universal, eternal
śānti: peace
sat: Truth
satsaṅg: in the company of a knower of the Truth (saint)

sevā: work offered as service to the Guru

Shaivism: philosophy based on the idea that all is
    Consciousness

siddha: perfected being

Śiva: Hindu deity, the primordial Guru

So'ham: natural mantra; literally, "I am That" [see *Haṁsa*]

spanda: creative vibration of Consciousness

śraddhā: faith

Śrī: name of Lakṣmī, also title of respect

sukhadaṁ: joy

Tukārām Mahārāj: [1608–1650] poet saint

turīya: transcendental state of Consciousness

Upaniṣads: ancient Hindu scriptures

Vedānta: philosophy based on the Vedas

Vedas: ancient Hindu scriptures

vikalpa: movement of the mind

viveka: discrimination

Yājñavalkya: ancient sage, appears in the *Upaniṣads*

Yoga Vāsiṣṭha: ancient Hindu scripture

BABA MUKTĀNANDA

MAY 16, 1908 - OCTOBER 2, 1982

Meditate on your Self.
Worship your Self.
Kneel to your Self.
Honor your Self.
God dwells within you as you.

MAHĀMANDALEŚVAR SWAMI NITYĀNANDA

Mahāmandaleśvar Swami Nityānanda is from a lineage of traditional spiritual teachers in India. While carrying the traditional teachings, he makes spirituality a practical part of modern daily reality, guided by the prayer "May all beings live in peace and contentment."

Born in Mumbai, India, in 1962, Swami Nityānanda was raised from birth in an environment of yoga and meditation. His parents were devotees of the famous ascetic avadhūt Bhagavān Nityānanda, and then became disciples of his successor, the renowned Guru, Baba Muktānanda.

Swami Nityānanda was trained from childhood by Baba Muktānanda and initiated into the mysterious path of the Siddha Gurus. He learned the various yogic practices, including meditation and Sanskrit chanting, and studied the philosophies of Vedānta and Kashmir Shaivism.

He was initiated into the Saraswati order of monks in 1980 at eighteen years of age and was given the name Swami Nityānanda by Baba Muktānanda. In 1981, Baba Muktānanda declared Swami Nityānanda would succeed him to carry on the lineage.

In 1987, Swami Nityānanda founded Shanti Mandir as a vehicle for continuing his Guru's work and subsequently established three ashrams.

MAHĀMANDALEŚVAR
SWAMI NITYĀNANDA

In 1995, at the age of 32 at a traditional ceremony in Haridwar, India, the *āchāryas* and saints of the Daśanām tradition installed him as a Mahāmandaleśvar of the Mahānirvani Akhara. He is the youngest recipient of this title since the inception of this order.

Currently Swami Nityānanda, also known as Gurudev, travels around the world, sharing the spiritual practices in which he has been trained.

SHANTI MANDIR

Shanti Mandir, a spiritual nonprofit organization, is dedicated to the preservation of Baba Muktānanda's teachings.

One of the ashrams of Shanti Mandir is near the banks of the River Ganges, at Kankhal, adjacent to Haridwar. The other ashram, at Magod, is in rural surroundings, amidst a twenty-acre mango orchard, in the state of Gujarat. Shanti Mandir's ashram in the United States is on 294 wooded acres outside the town of Walden, New York.

Under the guidance of Swami Nityānanda, Shanti Mandir symbolizes peace, progress, and love. In addition to the spiritual practices carried on daily, the three ashrams contribute their resources toward the following charitable activities: Śrī Muktānanda Sanskrit Mahāvidyālaya (education), Shanti Arogya Mandir (health), and Shanti Hastkala (economic opportunity).

LOKĀḤ SAMASTĀḤ SUKHINO BHAVANTU

MAY ALL BEINGS BE CONTENT

CPSIA information can be obtained at www.ICGtesting.com
Printed in the USA
BVOW010731081112

304981BV00004B/2/P